Department of Education and Science

Safety at School: General Advice

DES Safety Series No. 6

Other titles in this series:

No. 1 Safety in Outdoor Pursuits (Revised 1977)
No. 2 Safety in Science Laboratories (Revised 1976)
No. 3 Safety in Practical Departments (Revised 1977)
No. 4 Safety in Physical Education (Revised 1976)
No. 5 Safety in Further Education (1976)

London: Her Majesty's Stationery Office

First published 1977

Second impression (with amendments) 1977

ISBN 0 11 270441 7

Contents

Introduction

This series consists of six pamphlets each of which deals with a different aspect of the safety problem, No. 1. *Safety in outdoor pursuits,* was published in 1972, followed in 1973 by Nos. 2, 3 and 4, *Safety in science laboratories, Safety in practical departments,* and *Safety in physical education.* A fifth, *Safety in further education,* appeared in 1976.

Copies of all except No. 5 should be available in all middle and secondary schools, and aspects of No. 5 as well might be found relevant to sixth form colleges. The contents of Nos. 1, 2, 3 and 4 may also be found to be relevant to some extent in some junior schools. It is expected that one copy will be held centrally and others distributed to the appropriate department for the use of individual teachers. The pamphlets have been written with the day-to-day needs of teachers in mind; their purpose is to give guidance and to serve as points of reference for all educational establishments in which their contents are relevant. It must be emphasised that the activities described in *Safety in outdoor pursuits* and *Safety in physical education* are promoted by a wide range of establishments and organisations, statutory and voluntary, which provide for the education and recreation of young people outside school hours and beyond the statutory school leaving age. The advice they contain is therefore very relevant to all the sponsoring organisations and to further education establishments. *Safety in further education* (No. 5) and this one (No. 6) should be available in all departments in all colleges of further education whatever their particular function, with others in the series as relevant.

The present pamphlet provides advice to teachers on safety education and a general guide to safety precautions for all who work in the education service. It stresses the importance of care and forethought when designing and maintaining buildings and choosing equipment. However, all teachers should be aware of dangers that can arise from incorrect use of materials and equipment. One chapter gives consideration to the special needs of handicapped children and others deal with the two particularly serious problems of fire risk and road safety. Many of the hazards to which attention is drawn are to be found in infant and junior schools as well as in other educational institutions.

The many authoritative organisations concerned have been consulted during the preparation of these pamphlets but no claim can be made for comprehensiveness, nor are the contents intended for use in any legal connection.

The Health and Safety at Work etc Act 1974 extended the application of safety legislation to a wider range of employees than hitherto, including teachers and others employed in the education service. Pupils and students come within the category of persons other than employees liable to be affected. The standards for the protection of the pupils and students should not be less than those prescribed for the staff, and indeed the immaturity of young people may require additional safeguards in some circumstances. It is the purpose of this and other pamphlets in the DES Safety Series to emphasise the special attention that should be given to the safety of pupils and students.

Some activities may require expenditure on equipment or facilities if they are to be conducted safely. Whether that expenditure can be made will depend upon the funds available and the other calls upon those funds. What is clear is that an activity should not be undertaken unless it can be made properly safe, and if the necessary resources are not available then some other means should be found of providing, as nearly as possible, the necessary educational experience.

Marginal rules have been used in this reprint to indicate any significant additions to or changes from the first edition.

1. Safety Education

Before a child is old enough to go to school he has to learn to cope with the problems of standing upright, walking and running. He is exposed to many hazards at home and in play with other children. He learns by trial and error and should be safeguarded from serious accident by the care and guidance of his parents and the other adults around him. The natural instinct to explore and venture must not be suppressed, for only through experience can independence be developed. To remove all possibility of accident would be to prevent the child learning how to recognise and deal sensibly and confidently with hazards which are sure to arise in later life.

Among children the force of example is very strong and in childhood lifelong habits are formed. Carefulness and a sense of responsibility grow out of certain attitudes of mind which schools can help children to acquire. These attitudes are nourished by the example set by teachers and others whom the children meet. The safety of children in school depends not only on the observation of rules and precepts, but on the existence of relaxed and orderly patterns of behaviour. Safety education must aim to foster a growth of consideration for others, and this is promoted by teacher example and by forms of teacher intervention which encourage the considerate and restrain the thoughtless.

Safety education has, of course, to do with things as well as people. The attention given by teachers and other members of staff to the care of equipment in schools—whether it is young children's simple toys or sophisticated scientific instruments—is an important element. Young children will care because their teachers are seen to care; older children acquire a fixed routine. Because they derive satisfaction from using them efficiently, children learn to respect the qualities of materials and inanimate objects, and thus to handle them safely and with respect. Here too teachers and other members of school staff exert an influence by their actions even more than by their words.

Opportunities will occur in the work of schools for giving direct education in safety, and there are many examples of projects involving visits by experts such as police, road safety and fire officers, and factory inspectors. The aim of such safety education is to enable children, as they grow up, to become increasingly aware of the risks which surround them. They should thus be better able to assess degrees of risk and better equipped to take such preventive measures as are necessary to avoid accidents to themselves and to others. The most effective lessons in safety that a school can give are probably those which are incidental, forming part of ordinary teaching. In this way pupils should learn to accept personal responsibility, to assess risks and to protect themselves and others by using their own increased knowledge and experience.

Teachers of very young children and those who teach such subjects as science, crafts and physical education at any level have special responsibilities, but all teachers should be conscious of a general responsibility for children's safety.

Primary and middle schools

Curriculum innovation and the development of middle schools have led to the introduction of a variety of equipment and materials for science, crafts and home economics in primary and middle schools, sometimes used in purpose-designed areas or bays, but also in classrooms where no special provision has been made. Whatever the accommodation it is important for safe working that equipment and furniture should be arranged to allow adequate circulation space. Specialist work of this kind, and similarly physical education and outdoor pursuits, are sometimes organised in the middle school by teachers who are not specially trained for the work. Much of the advice in the Safety Series is relevant to such situations, particularly where sharp tools, electrical equipment, chemicals and physical education apparatus are involved. It is most important that proper safety precautions should be observed so that young children are not exposed to risks which would not be permitted by experienced specialist teachers working in purpose-built accommodation. Safe practice should be an inherent part of the teaching and expert advice should be sought. Sometimes in open plan areas there will be two or more teachers working with children involved in a variety of activities, some of which may demand particular attention or be of a potentially hazardous nature. In these circumstances the teachers will need to decide beforehand how best to oversee the various activities, and may need to agree on certain procedures and areas of responsibility.

Planning for safety

Issues relating to the basic structure of school buildings are not the concern of this pamphlet. Over recent years significant developments have taken place which have made the school environment safer. Teachers have been consulted about new ideas and architects have been helped by accounts of what children do in school, how they release their energies, and by knowledge of the materials, tools, and equipment they use. In general, improvement in materials and design have gone far to remove the causes of accidents, especially those arising from unsuitable flooring and glazing, dangerous obstructions and projections, and poorly-planned circulation. Well-designed furniture, glare-free lighting, comfortable thermal conditions and reduction in noise levels also help in the creation of a safe environment. Fire prevention and means of escape in the event of fire are factors inherent in the good design of schools and, like access to the school for road transport (including buses), must be carefully considered during the planning stage.

A modern school is of complex design, incorporating a variety of spaces, sometimes open plan and often used by adults and young people after or during school hours. Community and youth provision have added to the complexity of some school buildings. Users need to know what precautions are to be observed to ensure their safety in all circumstances and it is a wise precaution when any building (particularly an adapted or new building) is to be handed over, for the architect or his representative to inform the users how it functions and for the latter to consult with fire and safety officers about its safe use. Accidents which in spite of these precautions do occur should be investigated in case some undisclosed danger is the cause.

Teaching first aid

Direct teaching of first aid may well be introduced with older children in a junior school. The aim should be to enable children to recognise when an injury calls for expert attention. They should learn how to provide the immediate help which might prevent further injury and to understand the dangers involved in trying to move anyone seriously hurt. Older children should know how to treat for shock and to apply modern methods of resuscitation. The 9th edition of the *First aid junior manual* of the British Red Cross Society contains clear descriptions of modern methods of artificial respiration and of first aid for victims of electric shock, and schools should possess a copy. The British Red Cross Society and the St. John Ambulance Brigade have training schemes for young people over 11 and are prepared to give instruction in schools if asked.

Appendix B to each of Nos. 2, 3 and 4 of the DES Safety Series contains advice on first aid, including full details of the equipment that should be in every school. It should be the duty of one teacher in every school to check this equipment periodically and to ensure that the necessary stock of dressings and medicaments is maintained.

Training of teachers

There is a responsibility on those who carry out the initial and in-service training of teachers to include references to safety where appropriate. In some such courses safety and safety education may be incorporated in health education, in others an attempt may be made to treat the topic in a general manner by a series of lectures covering accident prevention. Both approaches have their disadvantages. On the one hand, by dealing with safety in too wide a subject context or, on the other, by treating it in isolation and failing to discuss its application to specific teaching situations, effectiveness and impact may be lost. A stimulating and relevant treatment can be to incorporate safety education in discussion of those areas of the curriculum, mainly the practical subjects, with which it is largely concerned; when that is done care needs also to be taken to encourage teachers to take an overall interest in promoting sound attitudes and behaviour in their pupils in all aspects of safety: on the roads, in the home and in their leisure activities.

2. How Accidents Arise

Many school accidents are trivial—bruises, minor sprains, cuts and the like. Even a minor injury, however, can cause a disproportionate shock and a serious waste of time, and injuries to the head should always be regarded as serious. Children differ widely in their susceptibility to accident and teachers should bear this in mind.

Playgrounds

Many accidents in school happen in the playground and arise from collisions and falls which are occasionally serious. Teachers know from experience how unavoidable some of these mishaps appear to be, especially among younger children. When breaks allow children of different age groups to use the playground space at different times the possibility of accident is likely to be less. Very young children, such as those in nursery classes, should have an area of the playground reserved for them. Attention should always be given to the security of the perimeter fencing of a playground used by the young.

Cloakrooms

There is a potential danger, especially to younger children, in the use of roller towels. Accidents arising from their use are rare but have sometimes been fatal. They can only happen if there is a sufficient length of towel exposed for a child's head to be inserted in the loop and for the towel to be twisted around his neck. Local authorities should ensure that the arrangements for towels and automatic towel dispensers do not present this risk, and should remind staff from time to time of the potential danger.

Outdoor equipment

It is especially important that the outdoor equipment provided for nursery schools and classes should be scrupulously maintained. This demands that all parts should be inspected frequently. Wheeled toys should be given special attention; spokes, for instance, can be dangerous. All wooden surfaces should be kept free from splinters. Not only the ropes but the seats of swings thus require frequent inspection. Outdoor sandpits need to be protected from dirt and from animals; some type of cover is therefore necessary.

Animals are often kept in schools, both inside and outside the buildings. It is essential to provide careful supervision of their handling and of the cleaning of cages.

Most other outdoor equipment is used in connection with physical education or the school garden. Reference should be made to the appropriate pamphlets in the Safety Series and to the appendix to this pamphlet dealing with poisonous substances.

Teaching aids

In nursery schools and classes indoor toys and play equipment should satisfy safety regulations. LEAs should be certain that their suppliers are aware of, and have complied with, these regulations.

Much audio-visual equipment is now available in schools and its proper use and maintenance are of the greatest importance. Circuits should not be overloaded and equipment should always be properly earthed when appropriate. Television sets with large screens intended for class viewing in schools are commonly mounted on stands so that the whole structure is a single unit. But the unavoidable top-heaviness of these assemblies is a source of serious danger to children and television trolleys should be pushed (not pulled) only by adults. (See Appendix D.)

Other heavy and possibly unstable equipment may be found in schools; for instance, upright pianos. Children should not be allowed to move any equipment of this type. Guillotines are also found in schools and can be highly dangerous. They should be adequately guarded when in use and kept locked when not in use.

Instruments for cutting paper and board are normally part of school equipment. It is sensible for schools to provide scissors with rounded ends for children up to 8 or 9 years old, but occasionally even young children need to use a pair with at least one side pointed. Risk can be reduced by the organisation of the work so that only small groups use sharp instruments at one time and are thus more easily supervised.

Fieldwork

In some instances fieldwork in urban areas, eg the study of shopping, housing, transport, urban growth and decay, may involve danger to pupils. Guidance about safety may also be needed for pupils engaged in community service in the neighbourhood. Teachers who take children on visits to farms should make themselves thoroughly aware of the hazards presented by farm buildings and machinery, by farm animals, and, in particular, by agricultural chemicals; and of the severe risk of rapid spread of fire in straw and hay. The number of children in the group should be small enough to permit effective supervision. Precautions should include a preliminary visit by the teacher and instruction of the children prior to the group outing.

Out-of-school hours

Leisure pursuits after school or during the dinner hour, and the use of the school, youth wing or annexe by young people and adults in the evenings and weekends, can involve some hazards not normal in school hours. Fire risks, for example, will be increased where smoking is permitted; or because a fault has developed in amplifying equipment, sometimes non-professionally made; or because fire exits have unwisely been locked to aid supervision. Ideally, doors across escape routes should not be fitted with locks. If however, to aid management, they are lockable, those doors which provide essential escape routes from occupied points of the building must, during the period of such occupation, be kept unlocked with the key removed.

Some health hazards can be avoided by insistence on high standards of hygiene: in the coffee bar, for example, by discarding all cracked and chipped crockery immediately.

As schools are often used by young people and adults after dark, external lighting and lighting on staircases should be adequate.

Where outdoor pursuits*, either on or off school premises, are arranged jointly by school and youth service, all young people involved should be adequately covered for insurance purposes, whether or not they are still in full-time education.

Reporting accidents

When an accident does occur a report should be prepared in accordance with the procedure laid down by the school or by the local education authority. Some apparently minor injuries, particularly those involving the face and head, can be followed by serious complications. If the legal responsibility for an accident has to be decided it is a matter for the courts; but the moral responsibility for the safety of the pupils lies with the school.

---

* See *Safety in outdoor pursuits,* DES Safety Series No. 1.

3. Special Precautions for the Handicapped

All the precautions outlined in this pamphlet apply even more forcefully to handicapped children, whether in ordinary or special schools. The teacher's aim is that each child should achieve as much independence as is compatible with his or her disability. This will depend on well thought out arrangements for protection against hazards and on continuing training in how to deal with them. No equipment should be used by children unless they have been, or are being, taught to use it properly.

Handicapped children may be insufficiently mobile to avoid danger or may have medical conditions which make them less aware than other children of normally obvious hazards. Thus there are special precautions to be taken where children with impaired vision or hearing are involved. There are other less obvious cases, such as those with spinal nerve lesions who may have large areas of insensitive skin, particularly susceptible to burns and pressure damage. Handicapped children are even more dependent on able-bodied adults for guidance and protection than are children without handicaps. Such adults should be available at all times; night supervision is necessary in boarding schools, and children should know how and whom to call for help if night-duty staff are not close at hand.

Fire and other heat risks

It is particularly important that full fire drills are carried out periodically as it may not otherwise be realised how much extra time is required to evacuate a school building or what additional provision needs to be made for those with difficulties in movement, hearing or sight. Additional responsibility is placed upon adults when dealing in emergencies with children of low intelligence. Special attention is drawn to Chapter 4, and absolute insistence must be placed on the provision of an effective fire guard for every 'open' gas, electric or solid fuel fire.

Christmas decorations may be a source of fire danger at home or at school, and extra precautions should be taken where there are handicapped children. Toxic fumes from badly operating boilers and stoves are particularly hazardous to children unable to appreciate or voice their discomfort or to take avoiding action, and any defect should be put right at once.

Underfloor heating (a feature of some nurseries and special classrooms where mentally or physically handicapped children may spend much of their time on mats) has been known to cause smouldering in a pile of stored mattresses. Care should be taken in the suitable storage of such equipment.

The danger of unguarded radiators is increased where there are children with skin insensitivity or other sensory defect, with mental handicap or with poor mobility. Free-standing oil heaters should not be used in such circumstances.

To avoid any risk of scalding by hot water, supplies to taps and showers should be maintained at the right temperature for washing without the need for mixing with cold. Children with poor hand control, for example, as well as those with the other handicaps already mentioned, may be particularly vulnerable if this precaution is ignored.

Fittings and equipment

An alternative supply of emergency lighting in key positions should always be available where there are children with severe physical or mental handicaps. Sometimes it may be necessary to arrange for an independent electricity generating service, but generally electric torches or some other form of battery operated lighting will do.

For physically handicapped children non-slip floors are vitally important, and there should be no hazards such as trailing electric cables. Special care is needed in overseeing the use of powered tools in craft rooms; in the home economics area special devices for those with visual or physical difficulties should be available and should be used, and the layout should be planned for maximum efficiency and safety.

Corridors should be kept unobstructed and projections such as coathooks should not be allowed to constitute a hazard to unsuspecting children. Ramps should be of suitable gradient for the use of wheelchairs and handrails should be provided, where necessary, in corridors and toilets as well as on stairs. The edges of paths and steps should be well marked and ornamental pools adequately guarded.

Lifts and special hoists may be used where there are physically handicapped children, and staff should be trained in their use as well as in the correct methods of lifting immobile children without risk of injury to either party. Lift doors should not be of the open trellis type, and where children operate the lifts, door handles and controls should be at a suitable level for operation from a wheelchair.

School transport

Transport arrangements are made for children attending special schools and frequently for handicapped children in ordinary schools. The vehicles should have safe doors and windows, and if wheelchairs are carried adequate anchorage should be ensured. A tail lift is an additional advantage. Adult supervision by specially appointed escorts is usually necessary. Physically handicapped children may have difficulty in balancing on seats and be particularly liable to fractures or other injury. The use of suitable restraining or seat belts is therefore recommended.

Deaf and partially hearing children may not hear vehicles entering the school grounds. A warning notice should be displayed for drivers.

Physical education

While every encouragement should be given to handicapped children to take part in physical activities, staff should be aware of the particular difficulties of individual children. Medical advice should be obtained where there is any doubt about the suitability of specific pursuits for individuals. For example, the written permission of the specialist concerned should be obtained before children with spinal defects are given the opportunity for horse-riding. Children at special risk, such as those with a history of epilepsy or of heart abnormality, will require additional supervision by staff aware of their problems, and the appropriate medical advisers should be consulted before such children are allowed to engage in physical activities.

Pools for swimming and water therapy should be planned and sited with the need for supervision and control in mind. Such supervision requires special attention where children with mental or physical handicaps or sensory defects are concerned, as no reliance can be placed on help from the other children in an emergency. For even a very small number of children there should always be at least two able-bodied adults, one to take emergency measures while the other goes for help. It must always be possible to summon aid quickly, and if other means are not available a telephone should be installed. The children should be under continuous supervision while they are in the building, including the time they spend changing.

Other hazards

Children with asthma, bronchitis and skin allergies may be hypersensitive to some of the substances used in school. Care should be taken with detergents. Animal fur can also precipitate allergic reactions. Handicapped children often derive considerable pleasure and benefit from handling livestock, but accidents may occur if the animals are handled roughly. There is therefore a need for supervision and for ensuring that children wash their hands after handling animals.

For very young handicapped children play areas should be designed so that there are no accessible electricity sockets or other hazards. Very small toys, or detachable parts of toys, which might be swallowed, should be banned, as should toys with sharp or projecting features. The danger from lead paint on toys or on furniture or buildings has been widely publicised, but this can still occasionally be a hazard for very young or mentally handicapped children.

The danger of roller towels has already been referred to. Many special schools use individual towels, particularly for boarding pupils. Children with most varieties of handicap should be able to use disposable paper towels, if necessary under supervision, in toilets and washrooms.

4. Precautions Against Fire

The following advice is based on that given in the Department of Education and Science Building Bulletin No. 7 *Fire and the design of schools**. That booklet deals in considerable detail with the designer's responsibility for safety, but design alone cannot ensure the safety of the building's occupants; any building can quickly become dangerous unless there is some foresight and care in its day-to-day use. Only the occupants can ensure that the building continues to be safe, and it is they who must know what to do if there should be a fire.

Suggestions for the integration of fire prevention teaching into the curriculum of schools are made in the Home Office publication *Teaching fire prevention* (HMSO, 1972). A teaching package for primary schools, *Project Fire* is also available.†

Action in the event of fire

A teacher's first and overriding duty in case of fire is, of course, to look after the children; no attempt should be made to fight the fire until their safety has been assured. Evacuation procedures will vary according to the design and type of individual schools. Evacuation should be carried out according to the procedures agreed in consultation with the local chief fire officer.

The fire brigade should be called immediately to any fire, however small, but small fires may also be tackled by the staff, using the methods appropriate to the type of fire. Laboratories, kitchens, workshops, craft and home economics rooms constitute areas of high fire risks. The right kinds of portable fire extinguisher (see p. 19) should always be available in these rooms and teachers should know how to use them.

Precautions throughout the school

Stairways and exit doors should be kept in good repair. No combustible material should be stored or allowed to accumulate in the stairway enclosures, and stairways and doors must never be obstructed. It must always be possible to open all exit doors easily and immediately from the inside while there is anyone in the building.

---

* 5th edition, 1975. HMSO.

† Free Publications, Home Office, Project Fire, P.O. Box 242, London SE1 0DE.

Ideally, doors across escape routes should not be fitted with locks, but where they are so fitted it is essential that they should be kept unlocked with the key removed for the whole time the building is occupied.

Fire doors, designed to delay the spread of fire and smoke, should be self-closing and marked with a warning notice that they are provided for fire safety. When possible these doors should be kept closed. The purpose of 'smoke stop' (type 2)* doors opening into stairway enclosures or across escape routes is to prevent blockage by smoke or dangerous gases. This should be explained to all the occupants of a school, together with the importance of ensuring that such doors are closed if there is a fire in any part of the building. These doors and all fire-resistant (type 1)* doors should be closed at night and during weekends and holidays so that if there is an outbreak of fire its spread may be contained and the damage from smoke limited.

In large open-plan rooms fixed items of furniture and equipment, such as those for cooking and science teaching, should be positioned where there is no risk of their forming hazards on escape routes. In all practical areas materials or loose furniture should not be allowed to accumulate and impede the movement of the occupants. It is essential that all pupils should have an unobstructed passage to the exits from such areas.

Rubbish and combustible waste should not be allowed to accumulate, particularly in laboratories, workshops, craftrooms and boiler rooms. Particular care should be taken with the storage of such material in caretakers' rooms and stage storage areas. It should be put in a metal or other non-combustible container and properly disposed of as soon as possible.

Every open fire (gas, electricity or solid fuel) must be provided with a fire guard complying with the appropriate British Standard Specification. Other heating appliances, such as convectors and storage heaters, may require protection to ensure that they are not misused, eg by blocking air grilles. Regular maintenance is strongly recommended.

Attention to electric cable and fittings is of great importance. Fuses must be replaced only with fuses of the correct rating, never of a higher rating or, as sometimes happens, with thick copper wire. Flexible cable fitted should be no longer than necessary and should be inspected regularly and replaced immediately if worn. Additions or alterations to wiring should be undertaken only by a competent

---

* BS Code of Practice CP3 (1968).

electrician. Special care should be taken over improvised stage lighting, amplifying equipment, and 'fairy lights' or other types of lighting used for decorative purposes.

Laboratories

Precautions against fire in laboratories are dealt with in Safety Series No. 2, *Safety in science laboratories.* Further guidance can be obtained from *Teaching fire prevention* (HMSO, 1972), prepared by the Home Office, Scottish Home and Health Department and the Central Office of Information, and from *Fire prevention material for schools,* prepared by the Fire Protection Association, 1968.

Hazardous experiments and demonstrations should not be carried out near the door of a laboratory or workshop.

The amount of petrol and other flammable liquids stored on the premises should be strictly limited, and any quantity over and above that in immediate use should be kept in a separate store detached from the main buildings. With petrol, there is a statutory requirement* that, unless its storage has been licensed by the local authority (who may attach to the licence such conditions as they consider appropriate) not more than 14 litres in the aggregate may be stored, in separate containers each containing not more than 0.5 litres.

Home economics rooms

Electric irons should be plugged into sockets fitted with pilot lights and always used with an efficient stand. Metal stands are acceptable if air can circulate below them, but thick mats of hard fireproof insulating material (not soft asbestos) are better. Flexible cable is frequently damaged by being put away wound round an iron that is still hot; irons should be allowed to cool down before being put away. Attention might be drawn to this point by suitable notices in home economics rooms.

Furnishings and equipment

Great care should be taken that any curtains, furnishings, or educational and display materials do not constitute a particular fire hazard. Fire-retardant materials such as woven glass fibre should be used wherever possible, but where these are not suitable, materials treated to make them fire-resistant should be used.

---

* By virtue of the Petroleum (Consolidation) Act 1928 (18 and 19 Geo 5 Ch 32) HMSO. Attention is also drawn to the Petroleum (Consolidation) Act—*Home Office model code of principles of construction and licensing conditions, part* 1 (HMSO 1968).

However, most furnishing materials and equipment available for use in general and specialist teaching areas are to some extent flammable. It is therefore essential, when selecting material to furnish a school, to give careful attention to the characteristics of the area in which they will be used. Advice might be sought from responsible organisations* as to the suitability of various materials for the purpose proposed and as to their compatibility with other materials in the school. Special care should be taken in areas containing a higher-than-average extent of plastic-based materials, eg laboratories and informal seating areas. With the greater use of mobile and loose furniture in schools it can be difficult to maintain clear unobstructed escape routes. It is, however, essential that such routes should be maintained and that through regular fire drills and the practice of safety procedures they become well known.

Advice as to the most appropriate fire-fighting equipment for each teaching area should be sought from the chief fire officer.

Temporary displays and collections

Great care must be taken when using paper or flimsy materials for decorating rooms, especially where heating is by any kind of open fire. Decorations and evergreens should not be suspended from light fittings. Fire in suspended and highly flammable materials spreads rapidly, and blazing pieces may drop over a wide area before everyone in the room has a chance to escape. For this reason, cotton wool and most plastic materials, particularly foamed plastics, should not be used in suspended decorations.

Fancy dresses and costumes are often by their very nature highly flammable, and the greatest care should be exercised when school plays or parties are being held. At such times open and portable fires are undesirable but if used must as always be adequately protected with fire guards. To minimise the risk of dresses and costumes catching alight, mirrors should not be placed above fires in rooms used for changing clothes.

A large quantity of plastic waste material collected for a teaching project will introduce a new risk unless properly controlled. Collections of newspaper, woollens or other materials for sale to boost school funds must be stored, even for short periods, in such a way as to avoid both the obstruction of exits and the risk of fire.

---

* Fire Research Station; Furniture Industries Research Association.

Vandalism

There is concern about the increased incidence of fires caused by vandalism after school hours or during holidays, often resulting in extensive material damage and the disruption of children's education. The opportunity for such acts of vandalism can be reduced by ensuring that doors and windows are properly secured after school hours and that flammable material is not left needlessly accessible to intruders. In some cases it may be worth installing equipment to detect intruders. Certainly special care should be taken when maintenance work, re-building or re-decoration are taking place.

Dual use of schools

Where school premises are used by members of the public, especially outside normal school hours, additional safety considerations may arise. Escape routes and exits should be clearly marked for the benefit of anyone not familiar with the lay-out of the building. Those responsible for such out-of-hours activities should be carefully briefed about the position of telephones, escape routes, fire alarms, and fire-fighting equipment. Substantial ashtrays should be provided in rooms where smoking is likely. Thorough checks should be made of all parts of the premises at the end of an evening or a session to ensure that no smouldering fires or cigarettes are left burning and that all doors and windows are properly secured.*

Inspections, drills and warnings

The chief fire officer should be consulted about the periodic inspection of school premises to ensure that escape routes are properly available and that no fire hazards have been introduced. Head teachers may wish to designate one or more persons to take a special interest in safety from fire hazards.

It is important to ensure that periodic fire drills (by which is meant practice evacuations of the building, not fire-fighting practice) are carried out in every school. Again, the advice of the chief fire officer should be sought on details. Clearly one such drill should take place soon after new occupants arrive at the beginning of the school year.

In schools of one storey with less than 160 children fire warning may be provided for by fire bells or sounders audible throughout the premises. Larger schools will require manually-operated electrical

---

* See free advice leaflet, *Fire safety check list for youth clubs, etc*, issued by the Fire Protection Association.

warning systems. All call points from which the alarm is sounded should be in prominent positions and preferably of the 'break-glass-release' type. Independent electric fire warning systems should be tested once a week and any fault rectified immediately. Tests, results and action should be recorded.

Fire-fighting equipment

Chief fire officers should be consulted about the nature and installation of fire-fighting equipment in schools. In most schools portable fire extinguishers are the most satisfactory means of dealing with fires involving ordinary combustible materials such as wood, paper and textiles. Soda-acid extinguishers, or those which expel only water, are suitable for fires of this type. For fires involving flammable liquids or cooking fat, foam, dry powder, or carbon-dioxide extinguishers should be used.

Buckets of sand are useful in a laboratory, particularly for the containment of spillages of flammable (or other) liquids. Nearly every kind of outbreak likely to occur can be dealt with by using sand or a suitable fire extinguisher. Buckets of water are of little use in fighting fire in a school.

Blankets are invaluable in dealing with people whose clothes are alight and can also be used to smother small fires involving cooking fat or other flammable liquids. They should be made of glass fibre or other material approved by the chief fire officer.

Extinguishers should be maintained and recharged according to the manufacturer's instructions. When in position they should be well away from any heat-producing appliance and should not stand in direct sunlight. Spare extinguishers and refills should be stored in a cool dry place and never in storerooms attached to classrooms.*

---

* British Standard CP 402: Part 3: 1964 *Fire-fighting installations and equipment—portable fire extinguishers for buildings and plant.*

5. Precautions in the Use of Electricity

Electrical appliances are an essential part of school equipment and the study of electricity properly forms an important element in science courses. This chapter deals with precautions which all teachers should exercise in the use of electrical equipment of any kind.

Fatal accidents are fortunately rare but the conditions from which they may arise are not.* School authorities and teachers should reduce these conditions to a minimum and take every opportunity to educate children to an awareness of the dangers involved and of the need for continual vigilance and care. The major risk is the danger of electric shock which at all times is unpleasant but which can be fatal, even with apparently innocuous voltages.

The severity of an electric shock is determined mainly by the strength of the current passing through the body and the path which it takes. Accidents do happen in which the body provides a direct connection between live conductors, as when the hand or a tool is introduced into equipment connected to the supply. Much more often the connection is between one live conductor and the earth through the floor or through adjacent metalwork. Metal, water and gas supply pipes, radiators, concrete floors and sinks provide ready conducting paths of this kind; the disposition of power points and equipment should minimise the risk of the body forming a link between the 'live' equipment and such earthed conductors.

A dangerous current can well be produced by 60 volts or even lower in certain especially sensitive individuals. Much depends on the nature of the contact with the live and earth conductors. Wetness or moisture at the surfaces (perspiration, for instance), or an increase in the area of contact, will lower the resistance and thus increase the current. Increased pressure increases the true area of contact in a way which is frequently not obvious.

Treatment of electric shock

The victim must be separated from the source of supply. If it is not possible to do this by switching off the current, rubber gloves, a dry mackintosh coat or dry woollen material should be used to

---

* About 200 people die each year from accidents involving electricity; many more suffer severe injuries, of which burns are generally the most serious.

protect the hands, and a dry mat or coat should be placed underfoot before the person is touched. A doctor or ambulance should be called at once. If no breathing can be detected a recognised method of resuscitation should be applied immediately, for example mouth-to-mouth breathing. If the pulse cannot be felt, and there is no other evidence of heart action, external heart massage should be applied as well. Efforts should be continued until medical help arrives or natural response occurs.

Installations and equipment

Electrical equipment in schools ranges from the fixed permanent installations for lighting, cooking, and crafts, to the temporary experimental circuits used for teaching purposes and referred to in *Safety in science laboratories*.* Within the range is included a wide variety of audio-visual aids and a number of semi-permanent installations, of which illuminated aquaria and lighting equipment set up for a limited period are common examples.

The fixed installations should be designed and approved by a qualified electrical engineer and they should not be extended or modified without reference to the appropriate authority. Compliance with the *Electricity regulations* (which are statutory) and also with the *Regulations for the electrical equipment of buildings* issued by the Institution of Electrical Engineers should be a condition of contract. This category includes such items as stage lighting and the heavier power-driven equipment in craft rooms, workshops and home economics departments. If the appliances are in regular use, they should preferably be fixed. Metal parts should be permanently earthed, and this connection should be regularly and frequently inspected by someone of appropriate technical competence.

A rapidly increasing amount of portable equipment powered from the mains is being used in schools—small power-driven tools, domestic appliances and audio-visual aids for example. Some of these can be the cause of serious accidents. Thus the firm grip on the metal part of an electric drill will produce the low-resistance contact referred to earlier and a breakdown of insulation in the equipment would set up the conditions for a serious or even fatal shock if the earth connection were not properly made. Some equipment is double-insulated, however, and designed to be connected safely to the mains supply with two-core cable.

---

* *Safety in science laboratories*. DES Safety Series No. 2.

Musical instruments which depend on electricity are often connected to the mains supply, and to amplifiers, by long trailing leads. There is extra danger when such equipment is used where people can move freely, and where plug sockets are in or near serveries with washing-up facilities. In older premises such areas are often inadequately served by plug sockets, and there is a strong temptation to use multi-adaptors. Their use in these conditions is dangerous and should be avoided.

In music departments the production of taped music may involve the use of two or more linked tape recorders, together with amplifiers or oscillators, either amateur-made (in or out of school) or as part of more elaborate proprietory electronic equipment. The interconnection of such apparatus and the use of instruments with electronic amplifiers needs special care. Mains frequency hum produced by earth loops should never be cured by removing the earth connections from the external casing.

Connections and switches

There needs to be constant concern for the safety of the connection between an appliance and the power point. Switches should *always* break the live lead, which should be coloured brown,* and in some instances a double pole switch should be used to ensure complete isolation from the supply. In fused plugs the fuse must *always* be in the live lead and there should be some clear indication, preferably a pilot light, when a piece of apparatus is switched on. The external metal parts of any equipment should be earthed. This, if done properly, would ensure that an earth fault in the apparatus will cause the fuse or circuit breaker to interrupt the supply. Earthing does not, however, make the inside of the apparatus innocuous and before any adjustment is made, even the replacement of a faulty lamp, the apparatus should be disconnected from the mains by removal of the mains plug.

Making a good earth connection is a vital part of the general installation and calls for specialised knowledge and full compliance with the *Regulations for the electrical equipment of buildings* issued by the Institution of Electrical Engineers. All single phase mains sockets should be for three pin plugs. Connection between the equipment and the plugs should be made with three core flexible cable of suitable current ratings. The cable should have a tough plastic or rubber cover except for some domestic aids (eg electric

* In older installations or equipment the live lead may be coloured red.

irons) where braided cable is suitable. Moulded rubber plugs are preferable to the brittle plastic type since they are less liable to mechanical damage. It should be noted that the colour coding of the conductors in the mains connecting cable fitted to electrical equipment of foreign manufacture does not always conform to British standards (SI 310 1969 colour code regulations) Brown: live (L); Blue: neutral (N); Green and Yellow: earth (E). The safest course is to change the whole connecting cable for one with colours conforming to this code.

Safety devices and precautions

Fuses and circuit breakers are important safety devices and in replacing them care should be taken to use the correct type and rating. It is desirable to keep a stock of suitable spares, but the cause of the fuse failure should always be known before deciding whether to replace.

Regular and systematic inspection and testing both of equipment and of connections is necessary. This calls for technical skill and training and it is essential that the authority responsible for every school or college should assign a competent person to the task. Records of all tests should be kept either in a log book or on an equipment record card. The interval between tests will vary in different schools but it should never be more than a year, and when the equipment is in frequent use it should be shorter.

Both because safety demands it and because he should always bear in mind the need to encourage sound habits in his pupils, the teacher should always take the prescribed precautions and in all he does he should demonstrate the need for the greatest care in dealing with electrical equipment. Electrical appliances should not be connected to the lighting circuit. On each occasion they are used, cable and plug connections should be examined for wear or displacement, particularly at the point where the cable is clamped to the plug. Old or damaged cable should never be used. Pilot lights must be working. In the wiring of semi-permanent installations such as aquaria, particular care has to be exercised to make them safe. The mains voltage should never be brought to an exposed contact by an extension lead. Unexpected heat in a plug or socket may well indicate a loose connection.

These are examples of possible sources of danger. The very rapid extension in the use of electricity increases the risk enormously and makes greater the responsibility which teachers have in preparing their pupils for its use.

6. Road Safety

The background to the problem

Traffic is a hazard all children have to cope with. There are five times as many fatal accidents to children of school age on the road as there are in the home. What is required is a responsible and effective partnership between parents, teachers and the road safety organisations to develop the necessary knowledge, skills and attitudes in children which will enable them to use the roads safely, as pedestrians or cyclists, and so to minimise the risk to others as well as to themselves.

In 1973, 848 children under 15 years old were killed in road accidents, 14,392 were seriously injured and 45,348 slightly injured. Among children of school age (5–14) in that year, 8,453 pedestrians, 2,010 cyclists and 94 passengers on two-wheeled motor vehicles became fatal or serious casualties.

The most common characteristics of fatal accidents involving children on foot are the actions of children in dashing into or across the road, crossing a road when the view is masked by a stationary vehicle, or crossing the road without due care.

Children are most likely to be involved in a fatal road accident as pedestrians between the ages of 2 and 7, and as cyclists between the ages of 11 and 14. Fatal cycling accidents are most commonly the result of collision with vehicles that are turning or overtaking.

In 1973, 46 per cent of all pedestrian casualties were aged 15 or less. But young people are also particularly vulnerable as motorcyclists and as drivers: in 1973, 50 per cent of fatal or serious casualties among riders of motorcycles, scooters or mopeds, and 11 per cent of those among car drivers were under the age of twenty.

These figures show the extent of the problem and how important it is for teachers to be fully aware of the vulnerability of all pupils to road accidents and to do what they can to prevent them.

Research into child accidents

Studies have been and are being carried out at the Transport and Road Research Laboratory (TRRL) in the hope that the causes of accidents can be more clearly understood. These include the use of film to record the behaviour of children in normal road situations on a test track.

The information obtained by one police force on road accidents involving child pedestrians has also been studied. Accidents happen to children on foot because of lack of attention, distraction, faulty judgment, impatience, or inability to cope with complex situations. Data already collected suggest that frequently young children cannot perceive or interpret the situation as a whole. Studies have been made of children's success in judging when it is safe to cross. Preliminary results show that about two per cent attempt to cross the road when a vehicle is too near for them to be able to cross in complete safety. In general, children seem to be less likely to notice a vehicle coming from the left than from the right.

The extent of children's exposure to risk at different ages, and the importance of skill in behaviour as a factor in pedestrian accidents, are being studied at Nottingham University. A Southampton University study showed the importance of listening for and hearing traffic sounds when children were crossing streets. Research in Sweden showed that children often fail to look all ways at road junctions and that some do not fully understand how to use a pedestrian crossing safely. Swedish studies have also shown that motorists and parents themselves are often insufficiently aware how unpredictable a child's behaviour can be.

A TRRL survey in 1968 provided some useful evidence of the type and extent of road safety activities in schools. A more detailed survey of driver and pre-driver training schemes was also carried out in 1968 and a report issued.* The principal conclusions from these surveys and other investigations into the effectiveness of various teaching approaches are mentioned where relevant in the following sections.

Pedestrians

Kerb drill was for a long time the most important item in child pedestrian training. However, this was criticised because it seemed inappropriate to modern traffic conditions in which the chances of finding a clear road are becoming less. It has also been shown that many children cannot tell left from right reliably until they are about 8 years old. The kerb drill contained no suggestions about how to select a place to cross the road and tended to be learnt by

---

* Reference LR 388 and LR 668, TRRL, Old Wokingham Road, Crowthorne. Berks.

rote, with insufficient emphasis on understanding, particularly of the need to adapt the drill to a variety of situations. There is some evidence that some children may have regarded it as a safety rite to be gone through before crossing the road, rather than a device for detecting and avoiding danger. Because of these inadequacies, a committee was set up in 1969 by the Royal Society for the Prevention of Accidents to review the kerb drill, and a considerable amount of research was carried out by TRRL to help in deciding what should be included in any new version, and to examine the best ways in which the new advice could be expressed. As a result of this the Green Cross Code was devised. It is:

First find a safe place to cross, then stop.
Stand on the pavement near the kerb.
Look all round for traffic and listen.
If traffic is coming let it pass.
Look all round again.
When there is no traffic near, walk straight across the road.
Keep looking and listening for traffic while you cross.

Attempts to evaluate the Green Cross Code's effectiveness when it was first publicised were encouraging. In the three months following its introduction and the extensive publicity given to it, accidents to child pedestrians fell by 11 per cent below what would have been expected. However, subsequent research and experience have shown that children, especially the younger ones, may have difficulty in recalling the Code. When the Code was being developed TRRL research established that its 13 pieces of advice could be used satisfactorily by children aged 7 and over.

Very young children find choosing a safe place to cross particularly difficult, although they can recognise and use protected places such as subways, bridges, pedestrian crossings and crossing patrol points. There is also evidence that children do not always look all round, but only right and left. This makes it all the more important that the code should be carefully explained and discussed, not just learned by rote. It is also important to secure the understanding and support of parents at this stage. Very young children may not be able to appreciate when an approaching vehicle is at a safe distance, as this involves ability to judge its speed: it may be best to teach them to cross, if they must cross when unaccompanied by an adult, only when the road is clear, unless they are at a protected crossing place. It is especially important that children should learn the Green Cross Code as soon as they are able to understand it properly, and use it in these limited situations so that good rather than bad habits form a basis for traffic education.

Children should be taught to cross at a distance from parked cars; that it is safer to cross where there is an island in the road; and that it is particularly dangerous to cross near a pedestrian crossing instead of on it.

In country districts, although traffic is less than in towns, there are hazards presented by the combination of the relatively high speed of traffic and unlit roads without footpaths. The need to wear something reflective or white at night should be stressed.

The school programme

Road safety teaching in schools can take two forms:

(i) a direct study of some aspects of road safety, usually by a series of lessons devoted to the subject; and

(ii) an incidental approach incorporating traffic education in other relevant topics.

Opportunities should be taken whenever possible to teach in real or simulated road situations by making use of the playground or a closed road adjoining the school. For the younger infants Tufty Clubs are particularly helpful. In Tufty Club meetings stories read to the children deal with many points which are important to all aspects of safety.

In the past the principal means of teaching road safety has been the enlistment of visiting experts; teachers have acted in supportive and organising roles. The greater difficulties which children experience in dealing with complex modern traffic situations call not only for new sets of general principles, like those set out in the Green Cross Code, but for teachers, in co-operation with parents, to play a more central role in the teaching of road safety. Thus schools should aim to develop in children a basic understanding of how to behave safely in traffic, and in doing this they will find it useful to draw upon the resources and expertise of police and road safety officers, who will make available films, demonstrations and other supporting material. To help teachers carry out this work in-service courses are valuable, enabling them to learn about up-to-date methods of teaching road safety. Several research projects are now in progress aimed at improving the road safety curriculum and developing teaching aids and techniques. Results will become available over the next few years.

Cyclists

Estimates from TRRL survey in 1968 suggested that 100,000

children of primary age (5–11) owned bicycles, though their use for travelling to school was often restricted. Training for cyclists is provided in both primary and secondary schools, although not necessarily for all the children who cycle to school. In about one-third of the schools in the survey the teachers carried out the training, the testing often being done by the police. Cycle training and testing are organised by ROSPA and, in 1971, 278,000 children were trained and 200,602 passed the National Cycling Proficiency Test. Until recently cycle training was limited to children over 10, but ROSPA have now introduced a modified scheme for children of 8 and 9.

In most cases the training takes place in playgrounds or other traffic-free areas, but a few schools provide some training and testing on the roads. Obviously stringent safeguards are required where this is done, and insurance implications need to be taken into account. Whether or not training in traffic is feasible, particular emphasis should be given to the need for careful observation; to the danger that other road users may fail to see cyclists; to checking that it is safe to make a manoeuvre; to giving clear hand signals well in advance; to the correct procedures for turning right; to dangers which arise from other vehicles turning or overtaking one another; and to the importance of proper maintenance of cycles.

The main dangers arise from other traffic, and the practical training can deal with these only to a limited extent. They are usefully covered in some detail in the classroom, perhaps with the help of slides or films. In teaching and testing cycling skills, as with pedestrian skills, advice and help can be obtained from the police and from road safety officers.

Motorcyclists and moped riders

Training schemes for riders of two-wheeled motor vehicles exist in many parts of the country, organised by the RAC and the Auto Cycle Union, and sometimes these take place in schools. Many pupils in full-time education ride motorcycles or mopeds. The frequency of accidents among such riders shows clearly the special dangers associated with two-wheelers, and schools will need to consider carefully whether they should discourage their use for travelling to school. This is a decision over which there should be consultation with parents.

But it is also essential that those determined to use a moped or motorcycle as soon as they are old enough should be given proper training in skills and attitudes. Legislation in 1971 raised the minimum age to 17 for motorcyclists, and this has resulted in many 16-year-olds driving mopeds as their first powered vehicles. Instruction in learning to drive these machines is vitally important. Schools may well find that the provision of this training is more appropriate to the interests and needs of older pupils, and to the facilities of the school, than driving courses using cars. At present only about 10 per cent of new riders of two-wheelers receive any formal training. Those who need further information about training schemes should approach the RAC or their local road safety officer. It is essential that such schemes should be properly covered by insurance and the appropriate LEA or other responsible authority must be consulted before two-wheeler training is started in a school.

Car drivers

An increasing number of secondary schools provide driving courses for their older pupils. The courses available take two forms: pre-driver training in which children who are not yet old enough to take a car on to a public road are given classroom tuition, and perhaps some off-road practical instruction in driving; and for pupils aged 17 or older, instruction which includes some driving on public roads. Sometimes the work is part of a CSE Mode 3 course in which road craft is a section.

The practical instruction is often provided by a driving school which has approved driving instructors and cars fitted with dual-controls. If teachers wish to give such tuition themselves the authority of parents should be obtained and they should be aware of the legal requirement that persons giving driving instruction for payment must be on the register of approved driving instructors held by the Department of the Environment. Whether tuition is provided from inside or outside the school, insurance must be discussed with the appropriate LEA or other responsible authority.

Police and road safety officers often help with courses on driving held in schools. Conflicting advice is possible if tuition is given by several different experts, and teachers organising such courses should be ready to help the pupils to resolve any differences. Even when no formal driving courses are held there may be opportunities to give general advice and information, as, for example, that injuries in most accidents will be considerably less severe if seat belts are worn by driver and passengers on all journeys.

The journey to school

The safety of children on their journeys to school is first the general responsibility of parents, but there are practical implications for LEAs and schools. All that has been said in this chapter about pedestrians, cyclists and the riders of two-wheeled motor vehicles is relevant to this issue. In addition, large numbers of children travel to school by bus and in private cars. There are particular dangers to children when alighting from vehicles and crossing roads near schools, and when standing at bus stops or on pavements or roads while waiting to be picked up. Where this is felt to be a significant problem (perhaps because of the numbers of pupils or because of local road and traffic conditions) schools normally give special attention to reducing the danger to pupils, either directly or in the course of more general road safety instruction. Pupils using buses should be reminded of the hazards of misusing automatic entry doors, tampering with emergency doors and of getting on or off moving buses. It also goes without saying that they should behave with due consideration for other passengers and for bus crews.

Teaching aids

The main source of teaching aids about road safety is the Safety Education Division, ROSPA, Cannon House, The Priory, Queensway, Birmingham, B4 6BS. Materials for use in Tufty Clubs can be obtained from that address, as can a variety of other aids for teaching pedestrian skills, including a set of slides and a record on the Green Cross Code, and a programmed text dealing with this code, produced jointly by ROSPA and the Automobile Association. Teaching material on cycling testing and training can also be obtained from ROSPA or through the local road safety officer. Information about moped and motorcycling training can be obtained from the RAC, the Schools Traffic Education Project, c/o STEP Management Services Ltd, Bristol House, Coventry Road, Sheldon, Birmingham, or from local road safety officers.

The journal *Safety education* is published each term by ROSPA, giving up-to-date information on the teaching of road safety, case-histories from schools, accounts of relevant research and information about new teaching aids. Six pictorial teaching aids, two each for infant, junior and secondary schools are produced each term by ROSPA and these give topical information about road dangers and ways of dealing with them. Normally these can be obtained through local education authorities.

The Information Services Branch, TRRL, Old Wokingham Road, Crowthorne, Berkshire produces a series of leaflets describing the results of investigations on road safety, which, particularly for secondary schools, could provide a source of ideas for projects and experiments.

Appendices

APPENDIX A

Circumstances of fatal road accidents to children under 15 in Great Britain, 1974.

Circumstances	*less than* 1	*years of age*														
		1	2	3	4	5	6	7	8	9	10	11	12	13	14	*Total*
Cyclists turning right								3			1	1		5	3	13
Cyclists failing to stop at major roads						1		2	1	4	1	4	1		2	16
Cyclists losing control				1			1	2				5	2	3	3	17
Cyclists colliding with vehicles —turning/overtaking						2	4	2	1	3	6	4	2	4	4	32
Cyclists with faulty equipment													1	1		2
Playing near delivery vehicles		4	3	3	4	1		1						1		17
Hanging on to moving vehicles (with or without cycle)							2		1		2	1	1	1	1	9
Losing control of toys								1	1							2
On footpath, verge		1	3	2		1		2	1	1	1	1	3	2	2	20
Zebra crossing with centre refuge									1		1			1	1	4
Zebra crossing without centre refuge	1			1		1	2		1	3	2	3				14
Running into road		3	12	21	22	31	27	28	23	18	14	14	10	5	2	230

Crossing road masked by moving vehicles											1		1			2
Crossing road masked by stationary vehicles		2	4	15	10	19	8	4	6	6	3	3	3	3	1	87
Alighting from bus (school/ public service vehicle)			1	1	1	3		1	1	3	4	2	2	3	1	23
Playing in street			1	2		1			1				1		1	7
Escaping from control of adults or older children			3	1	1	1										6
Crossing road to/from ice-cream van			2	1		1	2					1				7
Crossing road without looking (not running)		3	4	4	4	2	5	6	9	8	4	4	7	7	9	76
Passengers	5	6	4	6	7	7	7	2	10	7	11	13	7	12	10	114
Others	1	1	2	3	1	1	2	1		1	2	1		4	1	21
Totals	7	20	39	61	50	72	60	55	57	54	53	57	42	51	41	719

APPENDIX B

First Aid

All teachers should have a simple working knowledge of first aid, and it is important for them to be able to recognise when medical advice is necessary. It is also very desirable that some teachers on the staff of every school should have attended a course of training and taken a certificate in first aid issued by The British Red Cross and the St John Ambulance Brigade. The names of those so qualified should be made known both to staff and to pupils so that in the event of an accident first aid can be sought without delay.

The object of first aid is to give help at once to anyone who is injured or suddenly taken ill before expert help from a doctor or nurse is available or the ambulance arrives. It is aimed at saving life, preventing the injury from becoming worse, and helping recovery. Reassurance of the patient and protection from further danger play an important part.

Equipment

It should be the duty of one of the teachers trained in first aid to overhaul the equipment periodically and to ensure that the necessary stock of dressings and medicaments is maintained.

Fully equipped first-aid kits should be provided in every school and kept in easily accessible places. Teachers and pupils should know of their location. In secondary schools a kit should be kept in each laboratory, gymnasium, workshop and home economics room. In addition, pupils also should know the position of telephones in the school, and if there is one on the playing field they should know how to use it.

The contents of the first-aid kit should be simple and usable by any member of staff. A kit should include:

A pair of scissors (blunt-ended).
A few bandages of varying sizes.
A cotton triangular bandage to use as a sling.
Adhesive strapping.
A few packs of sterilised cotton wool.

A few packs of sterilised gauze for dressings.
A mild antiseptic solution.
Safety pins.

The School Medical Officer should advise on any additional items.

Epilepsy

During a major convulsion with loss of consciousness all that is necessary is, as far as possible, to keep the child lying on his side to maintain an airway and prevent suffocation from phlegm etc. This position is difficult to maintain during convulsive movements, but quite easy when they subside, and it is essential. During the convulsion it is best not to hold the child firmly, but only so to control him that injury from knocking into hard objects such as furniture is minimal. On no account should anything be put into the mouth—least of all the fingers. Side or face down position takes care of dangers from tongue-occlusion, and tongue-biting is rare. If micturition and confusion occur the child may need to lie down under observation for a while, but sometimes recovery is very quick. Most convulsions are over within a few minutes. If the convulsions are not over within about five minutes it may be wise to call a doctor. *Petit mal* needs no first aid.

APPENDIX C

Poisonous substances

The hazards that arise from the use of poisonous substances in science laboratories and practical departments are dealt with fully in the appropriate pamphlets of the DES Safety Series (Nos 2 and 3). Here attention is drawn to risks arising from materials which may be used in other parts of the school, including the school garden and swimming pool.

Teachers should be aware of the danger of certain substances of varying degrees of toxicity which are freely available and commonly used. Asbestos wool should not be used in schools, and the risk of exposure to dust from all other forms of asbestos should continue to be reduced by seeking substitutes wherever possible.* Benzene and other toxic substances should only be used in accordance with the advice given in Safety in science laboratories.** *Polystyrene* gives off toxic vapour when burnt or cut with an over-heated wire, and the dust produced when it is filed or sawn can be dangerous if inhaled. There are particular dangers arising in the use of kilns and also from pottery materials; lead glazes should not be used.†

Administrative memorandum 2/65 (as amended 14 October 1968) *Poisonous substances in pencils and other allied materials used in schools* and DES letter M30/33/03, 15 December 1972, *Poisonous substances in materials used in schools* give advice on various substances which may be contained in pencils, paints and other colouring materials unless adequate precautions are taken in manufacture. The Pencils and Graphic Instruments Regulations 1974 (Statutory Instrument 1974 No. 226) prescribe more stringent limits on the amounts of lead and other poisonous substances which may be present in the outside paint or core of pencils, pens, brushes, and similar articles manufactured for sale.

---

* See Administrative Memorandum No. 7/76.

**See para 101 *Safety in science laboratories*—Safety Series No. 2.

† See para 85 *Safety in practical departments*—Safety Series No. 3, and Administrative Memorandum 517.

Orthotolidine, which was at one time a reagent commonly used in kits for testing the chlorine residue in swimming pools, is now recognised as having carcinogenic properties.‡ DPD (*diethyl paraphenylenediamine*) is the safe and acceptable alternative now most commonly used. There may, however, be kits (possibly imported) which still include orthotolidine, and local education authorities and schools should ensure that they use only the safe alternative.*

Where the chlorination of the pool involves the use of *chlorine gas cylinders,* safe arrangements must be made for their storage and the proper precautions required when cylinders are being changed should be known and practised. The equipment should be handled only by people trained in its use. Suitable gas masks should be provided and kept at a convenient point adjacent to but not within the storage area. It should be realised that the accidental mixing of *hypochlorite solutions* and the *acids used to correct acidity values* produces highly toxic *chlorine gas.* The two substances should therefore never be stored together.

It is important that the concentration of chemicals used to control algal growths should not exceed that advised by the supplier. That is to say neither should the recommended amount of additive be exceeded nor should the volume of water in the pool be allowed to fall below that for which the amount of additive actually used is recommended. The build-up of concentration will be avoided if the pool is emptied and refilled with fresh water. It may be that in periods of restriction in the use of water some pools will have to be closed.

Certain imported musical instruments may have finishes containing toxic substances. It is suggested that acceptable toxic limits should be within those prescribed in the Toys (Safety) Regulations, 1974, although musical instruments are not controlled by these regulations.

Suspected toxic hazards can be taken up with the local authority analyst to whom the facilities of the Laboratory Consumer Hazards Analytical Information Service (CHAIS), Laboratory of the Government Chemist, Cornwall House, Stamford Street, London, SE1 9NQ, are available.

---

‡ See Administrative Memorandum No. 31/70.

* *Operation of small swimming pools.* Training manual for school caretakers. Local Government Training Board, 8 The Arndale Centre, Luton LU1 2TS.

APPENDIX D

Television receivers

Television sets used in schools should conform to safety standards at least as rigorous as those applicable to domestic sets and should incorporate additional safeguards against those hazards peculiar to their use in schools.

These requirements are described in detail in the British Standards Institution specification for *School monochrome television receivers and stands* (BS 4958: 1973, and Supplement No. 1: 1976). The paragraphs of particular relevance are: Sections 5 and 6 (pp 9-11) and Appendices A, C and D, plus the associated graphs (pp 12-22). Cross references are also made to other BSI specifications dealing with safety in television receivers. The recommendations can be summarised under two headings:

1. **Electrical safety requirements**

   The receiver should comply with the safety requirements of BS 415. It is important that the mains lead is correctly wired. On standard sets the mains lead may have a two-core cable but in some circumstances a three-core cable is necessary.

   Special care has to be taken when a television receiver is interconnected with other equipment such as a video tape recorder, and in BS 4958 this is the purpose of the specification for a television receiver 'with additional facilities'. Certain types of cassette video recorders are connected to the receiver on playback only via the aerial socket. Such interconnection is generally electrically safe when both the cassette recorder and the receiver comply with BS 415. But other video recorders in which connection has to be made to any other part of the television circuit must fulfil the special requirements of BS 4958 and will probably require the use of an isolating transformer. Such modification to a domestic or standard school receiver should be undertaken only by an electronics engineer fully conversant with the safety factors involved.

   Ventilation apertures should be gauze-protected in such a way as to prevent penetration and possible contact with a live part of the chassis. On domestic sets such protection is required (BS 415) for apertures on the top surface of the cabinet, but on school receivers such as those mentioned above it is recommended that *all* apertures should be gauze-protected.

2. Mechanical stability

Television sets with very large screens (measuring say, 60 cm to 70 cm) intended for class viewing in schools are generally mounted on stands so that the centre of the screen is not higher than 1.3 metres from the floor. It is essential that the set is securely attached to the stand so that the whole structure is a rigid single unit. If the assembly is to be mobile the stand should be mounted on castors not exceeding 100 mm in diameter and which cannot be locked.

For a stand without castors the complete assembly should not topple over when tilted to an angle of 15 degrees from the vertical in any direction. A mobile stand should only be pushed (never pulled) in a specified direction and this should be clearly labelled with an arrow on the assembly. When the receiver is moved it is recommended that it should be pushed only by an adult, not by a child, at a *very* slow walking pace.

With the wheels of the stand restrained from movement by small stops at the side or end nearest to the direction of tipping, the receiver and stand should satisfy the tests described in BS 4958. At right angles to the labelled direction of motion, the assembly should not topple when tilted to an angle of 15 degrees from the vertical. It is not possible, in this summary, to quote a maximum angle of tilt in the specified direction of motion, since a number of variables are involved. Reference should be made to BS 4958, Appendix C and Figs 5, 6 and 7.

The back of the receiver should be securely attached to the set in such a way that it cannot be easily or accidentally removed.

This advice also applies to colour receivers. It should be noted, however, that because of the extra heat produced in a colour set some of the ventilation apertures may not follow the recommendations of BS 4958 and the danger of touching live parts of the chassis with test probes is therefore much greater. The voltages involved are also much greater than with monochrome.

At the time of going to print (January, 1977) BS 415 is considered to be, if anything, slightly tighter than the equivalent European Standard IEC 65 (International Electrotechnical Commission). Negotiation is now in progress to bring about agreement between the two.

APPENDIX E

Lighting and excessive noise levels

Teachers, and especially youth and community workers, should be aware of possible hazards arising from excessive noise and from particular types of lighting peculiar to discotheques, since young people may wish to produce these conditions for themselves.

There is a possibility of damage to hearing from frequent exposure to excessive noise, especially if the levels are maintained for considerable periods of time. It is unlikely that the noise level in schools or colleges will exceed the levels laid down in the *Code of practice for reducing the exposure of employed persons to noise*, produced by the Department of Employment (HMSO). Despite this, however, every effort should be made to reduce the level of noise, especially from machinery. Advice is given in *Noise and the worker*, No. 25 in the Health and Safety at Work series.

The use of stroboscopic lighting of a critical frequency can produce photic epilepsy. Research into these problems is proceeding but in the meantime, and until more is known, it should be realised that these practices involve possible hazards to young people and that precautions to counter them may be necessary.

Index

Printed in England for Her Majesty's Stationery Office by U.D.O. (Litho) Ltd., London
Dd 586696 K80 12/77 S34924X/LE